Sing Freedom!

A Country Wins its Freedom Through Song

10% of every sale from this book will go to the Järvemetsa Scout Camp in Lakewood, New Jersey. This camp is for boys and girls and is supported by the Estonian American National Council, a 501c(3) organization dedicated to promoting the cultural heritage and interests of the Estonian people.

To learn more, go to www.estosite.org.

ACKNOWLEDGMENTS

Mike DeSantis

Jennie Levy

Kristin Blackwood

Sheila Tarr

Kurt Landefeld

James Tusty & Maureen Castle Tusty

Linda Rink

Mike Blanc

Marju Rink-Abel

Sing Freedom!
VanitaBooks, LLC
All rights reserved.
© 2015 VanitaBooks, LLC
No part of this book may be reproduced, stored in or introduced into a retrieval system, or transmitted, in any form or by any means (electronic, mechanical, photocopying, recording or any other system currently known or yet to be invented) – except by reviewers, who may quote brief passages in a review to be printed in a newspaper or print or online publication – without the express written permission of both the author and the illustrator, as well as the copyright owner of this book, Vanita Oelschlager. The scanning, uploading, and distribution of this book via the Internet or via any other means without the prior permission of the publisher is illegal and punishable by law. Please do not participate in or encourage electronic piracy of copyrighted materials. Your support of the author's and illustrator's rights is appreciated.

Text by Vanita Oelschlager. Illustration by Mike DeSantis. Layout & Production by Jennie Levy.

ISBN 978-1-938164-11-8 Hardcover
ISBN 978-1-938164-12-5 Paperback

VanitaBooks.com

Sing Freedom!

A Country Wins its Freedom Through Song

by Vanita Oelschlager
illustrated by Mike DeSantis

*This book is dedicated to
my granddaughter, Jamie.
I believe she will love to sing
like her mom and dad.*

Vanita

This is a true story about a small nation that won its freedom by showing that the spirit of a people is stronger than tanks and bullets. They showed their spirit by doing what they have always loved doing: raising their voices together in song.

Estonia is a small country located in the northeastern part of Europe between Russia and the Baltic Sea. It is the smallest of the three Baltic Nations, which also include Latvia and Lithuania. For much of its history, Estonia was controlled by other countries. By the 1920's, Estonia was free and independent, but that independence was short-lived.

Estonia's neighbor, **Russia**, was once part of a larger country called the Union of Soviet Socialist Republics (U.S.S.R.), or "Soviet Union" for short. In 1939, during **World War II**, the Soviet Union sent soldiers into Estonia. Estonia was then invaded by Germany, and again by the Soviet Union.

Many people were killed in fighting or sent far away to prison camps. Others escaped the war and fled to safer countries. By the end of the war, only three-quarters of the population remained, and much of Estonia was in ruins.

After the war, the Soviet soldiers did not leave Estonia, and it became part of the Soviet Union too. The Soviet Union, which was made up of Russia and fourteen smaller countries, followed a set of ideas called "communism," which controlled the way people worked and lived.

Under Soviet control, **Russian** became the official language, and Estonia was no longer treated as a separate country. They were not allowed to display the Estonian flag, and they were discouraged from singing their beloved folk songs and practicing their customs.

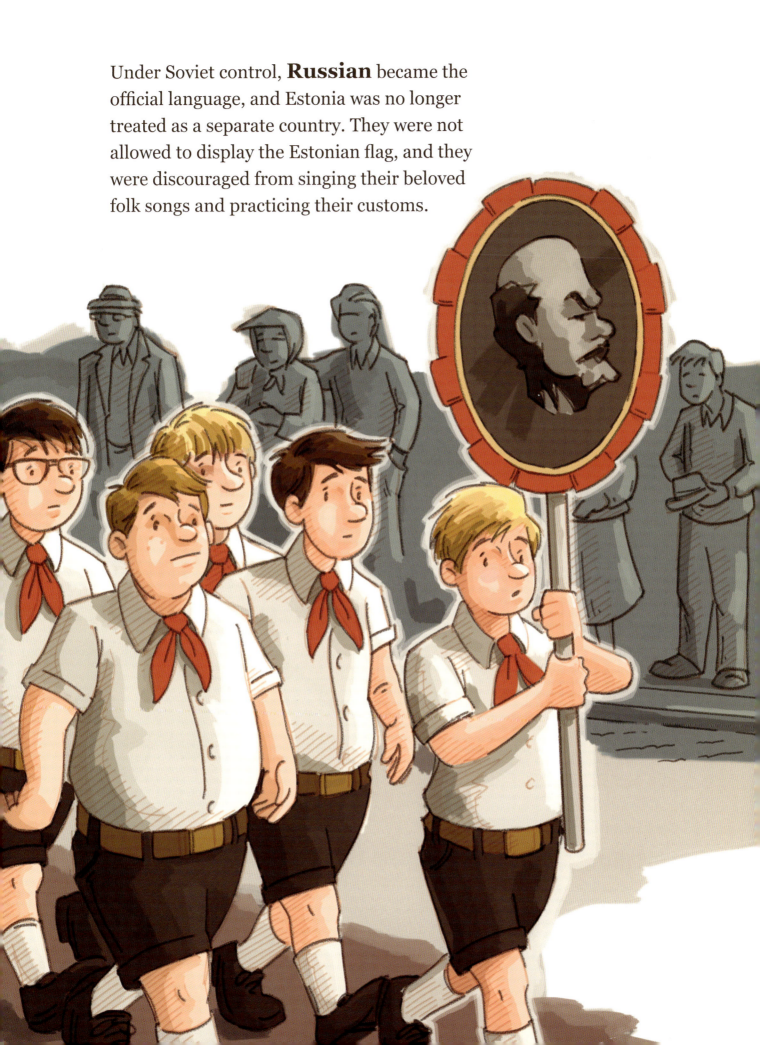

The Estonians were always afraid when the Soviets ruled them. They were not permitted to attend their churches. They lost their farms and businesses, and could be arrested at any time for speaking up against the government. Estonians became second class citizens and were forced to take lower paying jobs.

The Estonians had a long tradition of singing, and there was a national music festival called the **Laulupidu** that was started in 1869. Singing groups from all over the country would practice a set of songs. They would dress in colorful, traditional folk costumes and come to sing these songs together – often with over **30,000** singers!

The Soviets allowed the Estonians to have their festival in **1947**, but all of the traditional Estonian songs were replaced with Soviet patriotic songs in Russian. The Soviets checked the program, but one Estonian song slipped through, *Land of My Fathers, Land That I Love*.

Land of My Fathers brought the Estonians great pride and reminded them of their freedom, but the Soviets did not like it and did not let Estonians sing it after 1947. **In 1960,** the Estonians decided to take a chance.

The Song Festival started with the usual Soviet patriotic songs, but at the end of the program, the choirs of Estonian voices refused to leave the stage. They started singing **Land of My Fathers!**

The Soviets tried to have the band play loudly so that no one could hear it, but tens of thousands of singing Estonians could not be stopped! From that day forward, *Land of My Fathers* would always be sung at the Song Festival!

In 1985, Mikhail Gorbachev became leader of the Soviet Union, and he began to give people more freedom. Programs called Glasnost and Perestroika allowed for more openness and freedom of speech.

The Estonians used this new freedom carefully. They began to talk about their history and celebrate their culture. When no one was arrested, they began to gain confidence. They even talked about making changes to the government.

People began to sing Estonian songs at gatherings and festivals, and they wrote new songs to protest Soviet rule. They brought out Estonian flags that had been banned for more than forty years. The demonstrations grew and grew.

At the **Song of Estonia** festival, they sang songs, gave speeches and waved their flags. Nearly 300,000 people participated – about one quarter of all the people in the country!

The other Baltic countries joined in acts of defiance. Over **1,000,000 people** from Estonia, Latvia, and Lithuania joined hands to form a human chain across their countries from the city of Tallinn in Estonia to Vilnius in Lithuania. They joined hands in love and not violence.

But the Soviet Union was finished. Russia and other republics declared their independence too. The Soviet soldiers left the country peacefully. Estonia had already taken steps to elect a prime minister, restore Estonian as the official language, and remove restrictions on flying their flag. **Estonia was free,** and not a single drop of blood had been shed!

Today, Estonia is prosperous and free. In 2006, one study named Estonia the freest country in the world (the United States was eighth). Their capital city, Tallinn, is one of the best-preserved medieval cities in Europe, yet it is not a museum, it is a town where people live. You can feel history just by walking down the streets.

During Estonia's fight for freedom, an artist named Heinz Valk called the fight "The Singing Revolution," and said, "One day, no matter what, we will win!" Through their songs and peaceful demonstrations, the Estonian people did!

Glossary

Baltic Countries. The three small countries bordering the Baltic Sea in northeastern Europe: Estonia, Latvia, Lithuania.

Estonia. ("Ess-TONE-ee-ah") The northernmost Baltic country. 17,413 square miles (about the size of New Hamsphire and Vermont). It has a population of about 1,300,000.

Tallinn. ("TAH-leen") The capital of Estonia. Population 432,000.

Latvia. ("LAHT-vee-ah") The middle Baltic country. 24,938 square miles (about the size of West Virginia). It has a population of about 2,000,000.

Riga. ("REE-gah") The capital of Latvia. Population 643,000.

Lithuania. ("Lith-ooh-ANE-ee-ah") The southernmost and largest Baltic country. 25,212 square miles (about the size of West Virginia). It has a population of about 2,900,000.

Vilnius. ("VILL-nee-us") The capital of Lithuania. Population 540,000.

Soviets. ("SO-vee-ets") The name given to representatives of the former country known as the Union of Soviet Socialist Republics (U.S.S.R.), also known as the Soviet Union. It came into being as a result of the Russian Revolution of 1917. It was formally dissolved in 1991. From 1940 to 1991 the Baltic countries were part of the U.S.S.R.

Communism. ("COM-mun-izm") A political system by which most industries and land are owned and managed by the government in the name of the people. Virtually all countries that used to have communist governments have restored private ownership of property and varying degrees of personal freedoms.

Laulupidu. ("LAH-loo-PEE-doo") The Estonian singing festival held every five years that became a focal point for resistance to being part of the U.S.S.R.

Mikhail Gorbachev. ("Meh-KILE GOR-bah-shoff") The last premier of the Soviet Union. He began a series of reforms in response to growing unrest, but was unable to prevent the collapse of the U.S.S.R.

Glasnost. ("Glaz-NOST") A policy of increased government openness instituted by Mikhail Gorbachev. During its short period in the late 1980s, there was less censorship and greater freedom throughout the U.S.S.R.

Perestroika. ("Pair-ess-TROY-kah") A policy of restructuring the economy within the Soviet government that allowed for more freedom and independence.

Estonia is the birthplace of **Skype**, the software that makes online voice and video conversations possible. It is a technologically inventive country that some people call E-stonia. There are booths in the airport offering free Skype connections.

The Author

Vanita Oelschlager is a wife, mother, grandmother, philanthropist, former teacher, current caregiver, author and poet. She is a graduate of Mt. Union College in Alliance, Ohio, where she currently serves as a Trustee. Vanita is also Writer in Residence for the Literacy Program at The University of Akron. She and her husband Jim received a *Lifetime Achievement Award* from the National Multiple Sclerosis Society in 2006. She was named *National Volunteer of the Year* by the MS society in 2008. She was honored as 2009 *Woman Philanthropist of the Year* by the Summit County United Way. In May 2011, Vanita received an honorary Doctor of Humane Letters from University of Mount Union. Vanita and her team help young budding authors and illustrators write and illustrate their own books with the LeBron James Foundation's Promise Authors program. In 2014 she was named one of the *Women Trailblazers* by the Multicultural Center at the University of Akron.

Prior to her publishing and writing career, Vanita taught school for 19 years and then helped her husband with his company, Oak Associates. She is a mother of two daughters, stepmother to a son and daughter, and grandmother to nine.

The Illustrator

Mike DeSantis creates puzzles and illustrations for children's books and magazines. He attended the Cleveland Institute of Art and received a BS in Management from Case Western Reserve University. Mike lives near Cleveland with his wife, three wonderful children, and two barking dogs.

About the Art

STEP ONE

The pictures are first sketched on paper.

STEP TWO

The pictures are scanned into the computer, and the final lines are drawn using a digital pen, using reddish brown and dark gray.

STEP THREE

Light and dark areas are planned out.

STEP FOUR

Color is added to finish the illustration.